MANAGING
SUDDEN CHANGE
— in your —
CAREER
JOURNEY

SOLA OSINOIKI

Copyright © 2024 by Sola Osinoiki

All rights reserved. This book or any portion thereof. may not be reproduced or used in any manner whatsoever without the express written permission of the publisher except for the use of brief quotations in a book review.

All pictures are used with consent.

Paperback ISBN 979-8-9893893-2-2

ACKNOWLEDGMENTS

Not sure about you, but I have always had an aversion to having my creative writing edited. When I embarked on my journey as an author, every edit felt like a surgical intrusion. Over time, my chief editor has often reminded me that the intention is simply to bridge the gap between what my heart wants to convey and what my fingers or hands have written. It dawned on me that being married to my chief editor, Morounkunbi, is a privilege (it took some time to acknowledge this). She not only understands me but also aids in expressing my thoughts. To Morounkunbi, my editor-in-chief, greatest fan, and loving critic, I sincerely appreciate you accompanying me on this life journey! Nearly three decades of marriage and an even longer friendship journey. And the gifts of 5 amazing children!

One of the most significant roles in my life is that of a father. I love my kids and each one brought sudden change into my life. I learnt long ago that my role as a father is as a caretaker because every child belongs to God; they are a gift from Him and we have the privilege to act as custodians for a little while. It is truly a sudden change when you father four kids directly, and inherit an amazing daughter in love. Embracing this sudden change has brought me immense joy, and I consider it a tremendous privilege to be addressed as "Father."

So, to my children Olu, Funsho, Ola, Lola and Ayo (deceased), I express my gratitude for the valuable lessons you have taught me, and continue to teach me through your individual life journeys and the courage you demonstrate in managing sudden change in your lives each day!

This book is also a testament to the numerous remarkable companies I have worked for, and the awesome colleagues, managers, leaders, mentors, and coaches that I have met on my career journey, everyone of whom has contributed, directly or indirectly to the crafting of this book.

I am grateful for the twists and turns and the unexpected changes that I have encountered in my personal journey. Change is an ever-present force in the world and a certainty in the workplace, and is the inspiration for this book. As I share my personal stories of how resilience and adaptability in the face of change, has had a positive impact on my professional and personal growth, my hope is that this can be your experience too.

My deepest thanks to everyone who took the time to read the original drafts and add their valuable stories and comments. Thanks to Victor Olushola Kehinde, Rumbidzai Muteswa and Ndimofor Aretas. Thanks also to the amazing Black In Tech Berlin community for all that you have added to me.

Finally my thanks to Almighty God for giving me life!

Sola Osinoiki

TABLE OF CONTENTS

Introduction 9

My Stories of Sudden Change 15

Lessons from the Life of Joseph 27

Leading Self 33

The Seven Elements 37

Conclusion 57

Reflections 63

Reflections and Comments by Reviewers 69

INTRODUCTION

A SUDDEN CAREER change can be described as a pivotal moment when one encounters a substantial and unforeseen shift in their professional trajectory. This upheaval may manifest as a change in employment, a shift in job responsibilities, a transition between industries, or a complete realignment of one's overall career direction. The ripple effect might even extend to necessitating a geographical relocation. These transformative shifts can be triggered by a myriad of factors, including but not limited to workforce downsizing, shifts in personal circumstances, evolving priorities, the pursuit of fresh challenges or opportunities, or a redirection of industry focus.

As life is constantly evolving, one needs to embrace the need for adaptation. This may entail acquiring novel skills, redefining professional roles, or, in some instances, embarking on a fresh start. In the realm of "Sudden Change", it's important to be agile, and to adopt a reflective and proactive stance in order to effectively navigate and adapt to the unexpected.

While such change can bring about unexpected growth, it can also pose considerable challenges. It may take a long time to adjust to the impact of the change. Therefore, it is essential to recognize that Sudden Change is a personal and individual experience that can have both positive and negative outcomes. In this book, we aim to explore this concept in detail.

The global pandemic, for instance, is a prime example of a sudden change that impacted the entire world. In his book "The Winning", Tim Grover describes how the National Basketball Association of the United States (NBA) was impacted by the pandemic. He discusses how it affected the mental health and careers of the players; some grew and thrived during the pandemic while others tanked.

Similarly, sudden changes can occur in the business world, such as the sudden exit of a CEO, loss of funding for a startup, a major product modification or a product recall.

Personal sudden changes may arise from external sources, such as unexpected promotions or demotions, redundancies, departmental changes, relocation, or dependence acquisition. Other personal changes may not be work-related, such as a growing family, experiencing an empty nest, relationship changes, or loss of a loved one.

I will begin by sharing the story of one of my many sudden changes.

In the early stages of my career, I found myself at an unexpected juncture. After completing my education in Civil Engineering in Nigeria, I travelled to the United Kingdom to join my then girlfriend, now spouse, who had recently relocated there.

I tried to find work as a Civil Engineer, however, despite my qualifications, opportunities in my field proved elusive.

Determined not to resort to state support, I felt compelled to swiftly pivot and forge an entirely new career.

In retrospect, this decision proved to be a transformative and ultimately fortuitous one. It involved moving into a space where I had to teach myself computer programming.

This was long before the days of YouTube or ChatGPT. I taught myself how to program using Visual Basic while also working as a security guard so I could put food on the table.

On the back of the skills that I acquired, I was able to get a white collar job as an Analyst Programmer at the College of Law in Guildford, and the rest, as they say, is history.

Managing a sudden career change requires a certain level of grit and resilience. Unexpected shifts in one's professional journey can either catapult one towards growth and triumph or trigger a downward spiral of confusion and upheaval.

At the heart of this equation is the capacity to adapt, navigate, and master these transitions. One's true strength emerges in the reaction to such circumstances. It is our duty to focus our energies on the aspects of the change within our control, directing our efforts into purposeful and constructive endeavours.

This approach is integral to effective personal change management and, ultimately, career advancement. "The one thing you can truly control in any change or disruption is your attitude and your reaction."

MY STORIES OF SUDDEN CHANGE

IN MY CAREER, I have experienced several instances of sudden change that have forced me to adapt and pivot into new directions. My move to the United Kingdom as earlier mentioned, necessitated a change in my career, away from the familiar world of Civil Engineering to the uncharted waters of software development.

I attribute much of my career success to the support and guidance of my mentors over the years, whose counsel proved invaluable during these transitional periods.

Having landed my first computer programming job, my professional journey encountered another abrupt change one day, when I was faced with the threat of my job being outsourced to India.

I seized the opportunity arising from this unexpected turn to reshaping my career trajectory

These unforeseen events constitute integral aspects of the consulting landscape, presenting challenges that demand adaptability and strategic navigation.

For me, my Sudden Change on a consulting project happened while working on a challenging consulting project in the vibrant city of Manchester, UK. I found myself facing another unexpected twist in my professional journey – an abrupt termination from a project I had poured my dedication into.

Allow me to paint the picture for you: I was enlisted as a troubleshooter for a project that had veered off course and required immediate intervention and rectification. I uncovered the issues that came mainly from the complexity of the project as it was a joint venture project and so too many stakeholders and our job as consultants to try to find alignment. In my discovery I found the issues and was called to present to the body. The two project leads on the client's side start to say that the issue with the project was me. At one point the chair of the project board based on the evidence 'You are the weakest link'. She then dismissed the board of about 25 people and asked me and the executive to stay back and I was terminated and asked to leave the site.

The circumstances surrounding the termination were unjust and the way I was terminated was humiliating, but rather than succumb to the initial shock and disappointment, I resolved I would not allow this setback to define my future.

I kept my cool, managed my emotions and maintained unwavering professionalism in my interactions with colleagues as I was walked off the building. I recognized that how I reacted in the moment, could set the tone for the next step in my career journey.

So rather than focus on preserving my reputation, I responded to the situation with grace, cordiality and determination.

I didn't allow bitterness to take root, rather I focused on learning and growing from the experience. This commitment to keeping my composure, even in the face of a humiliating and unjust setback, became the catalyst for an unexpected turn of events.

My professionalism and resilience caught the attention of the project leaders in my firm, leading to an invitation to rejoin the project in a different capacity in a matter of days. The new role I was offered came with increased autonomy – a testament to the strength derived from facing adversity head-on. The experience illustrates the power of having a flexible mindset and mental fortitude. Add bonus I got an apology from the board members who created the confusion

This story is not just about overcoming a setback; it's about emerging stronger and more empowered.

My intent is to inspire you to view unexpected challenges as opportunities for growth. In the unpredictable landscape of professional life, your ability to navigate setbacks with poise and resilience, not only preserves your professional standing but also propels you toward greater achievements.

I can recall another instance of sudden change that catapulted me into a new realm of possibilities. It all started with a sudden double promotion that I was given, following the departure of my line manager. This wasn't just a career shift; it was a seismic leap into a significant leadership role in the bustling city of Philadelphia.

Stepping into the shoes of my boss so suddenly was both exhilarating and daunting. The enormity of the responsibility could have been overwhelming, but instead, it became a catalyst for monumental growth. The unexpected turn of events infused me with a surge of confidence and fortitude.

Navigating the challenges of this big leap wasn't always easy, but with each hurdle, I discovered layers of resilience within myself that I never knew existed. The pressure to lead fuelled my determination, and every decision I made became a stepping stone toward personal and professional empowerment. I also had the opportunity to work in the United States, which, I think, is one of the reasons I love to travel so much.

This career pivot didn't just mark a moment in time; it set the course for a decade-long adventure in consulting. Through the twists and turns, successes and setbacks, I cultivated a deeper understanding of my own strengths and abilities. The crucible of leadership honed my skills, and the furnace of change revealed facets of my character that became the cornerstone of my success. Needless to say, I had the support of amazing mentors who kept me focused.

Sometimes, the most significant advances in one's career can emerge from unexpected and challenging places. So, if you are standing at the precipice of change, let this be an assurance that daunting transitions can be the launching pads for unparalleled growth and self-discovery.

My third experience of sudden change happened a few years later while I was working in a consulting firm. A sudden notice period cut short my tenure at the firm, and my initial response was defensive and combative. However, with the help of my mentor, I was able to reframe this experience in a positive light and leverage my network to secure a new opportunity still in consulting, just three days later.

In all, I spent a total of ten years in consulting, however, my eventual exit from the consulting world was my fourth experience of sudden change. One fateful day, my line manager, out of the blue, introduced someone new to take over my role, prompting my unexpected exit. The standard six-month notice period was compressed to just two. I was unceremoniously thrust into the job market, scrambling to secure a new position.

In the midst of this uncertainty, a valuable contact extended a lifeline, presenting a short term opportunity within their organization. Little did I know that this unexpected twist would unlock an avalanche of thrilling prospects for me.

I end this chapter with an experience that has etched itself into the very fabric of my being. It unfolded in the wake of an indescribable loss – that of our second child. As I grappled with the heaviness of grief, I returned to work, seeking solace, and understanding. Little did I anticipate the callous response that awaited me from my boss, a response that cut through the rawness of my emotions.

In a moment where empathy should have prevailed, my boss, insensitive to the depths of my pain, suggested that tragedies were commonplace and that I should "get over it" and swiftly return to the rhythm of work. It was a chilling revelation of a corporate culture that often overlooked the humanity of the employee.

This experience was the catalyst for a profound shift in my perspective on what's important in life. It helped me reassess my priorities and I started to work towards achieving a more sustainable work-life balance. I also realised that the workplace should be more than just a space for professional duties; it should embrace the humanity of its workforce.

As a result of this personal tragedy, I became a determined advocate for colleagues facing similar challenges, committed to championing compassion and understanding in the workplace.

I started to mentor others who found themselves navigating the intersection of personal loss and professional responsibilities. I resolved to be a beacon of support and empathy, a testament to the belief that compassionate leadership can thrive even in the most challenging circumstances.

So, for those who may find themselves at the crossroads of personal trials and professional demands, let my story be a source of inspiration. Let it stand as a testament to the fact that resilience can be summoned in the face of adversity. Advocating for a more compassionate workplace can have a hugely positive impact on individuals and on the collective spirit of an organization.

LESSONS FROM THE LIFE OF JOSEPH

THE TIMELESS TALE of Joseph from the Christian Bible is a constant source of inspiration for me. His story is told in the book of Genesis, chapters 37-50.

Joseph's journey was marked by resilience and tenacity, and it began with a cruel and unexpected betrayal – being sold into slavery by his own bro-thers at a tender age. Yet, despite this unimaginable cruelty, Joseph's unwavering determination pro-pelled him to unprecedented heights, eventually securing his position as the de facto Prime Minister / CEO of Egypt. He became the right-hand man of Pharaoh.

Joseph was a master disrupter. I'll explain.

Firstly, envision the scene – an imminent famine threatens the survival of an entire nation. Joseph doesn't succumb to panic at the prospect of the looming crisis; instead, he becomes a master innovator, and strategist, crafting a revolutionary plan that would result in a massive food storage project that lasted an astounding 14 years.

This is no small feat, and required a level of foresight that set him apart from everyone else in Pharaoh's administration. Joseph had an incredibly broad breadth of his responsibilities, demonstrating not only his foresight but also his ability to navigate and lead in diverse domains.

This story is more than a tale of triumph over adversity; it is a masterclass in adaptability, creativity, and a willingness to challenge the norm. Joseph's journey reminds us that life and work are rife with sudden changes, demanding not only resilience in the face of upheaval but also the audacity to innovate and take calculated risks.

Joseph's story has reverberated down the centuries and continues to be relevant today, urging us to embrace challenges that come our way with an open mind and a bold spirit. In an era where disruption is the hallmark of progress, Joseph's story is a shining light, encouraging us to cultivate adaptability, nurture creativity, and fearlessly challenge the status quo. A timeless reminder that, even in the face of the most unexpected twists, our ability to evolve and innovate can pave the way for extraordinary achievements.

As a data-driven professional, I find Joseph's approach to strategy and problem-solving par-ticularly inspiring. Like Joseph, I believe that success often comes from disrupting conventional thinking and innovating new solutions to complex challenges. This mindset has guided me throughout my career, and I look forward to continuing to learn and grow as a disruptive professional in the years to come. There is indeed a big difference between a growth mindset and a fixed mindset.

In the unpredictable landscape in which many businesses exist, proactive preparation for un-foreseen change is paramount. One must be ready to react to unexpected shifts in the market, changes in industry dynamics, or in-ternal organizational structures. Embracing a growth-focused mindset is critical in navigating these changes.

Given that change is inevitable, personal development emerges as a critical linchpin if one is to survive sudden change. The world is in a constant state of flux underscoring the importance of continuous development. By prioritizing personal growth, individuals not only fortify themselves for the challenges of the present but position them-selves for the opportunities that will emerge as a consequence of the change.

Three main strategies are critical to managing sudden change:

i. Maintain a positive outlook

ii. React effectively to shifting circumstances

iii. Prioritise personal development

Adopting these three strategies together not only equips you to weather sudden change in the business environment but also sets the stage for continuous growth and adaptation in the ever-evolving professional arena.

As we contemplate the layers of Joseph's story, let it be a source of inspiration for our own endeavours. In the face of our challenges, may we find inspiration to construct our foundations, sell our visions with passion, analyse our situations with wisdom, and navigate diverse domains with resilience. Joseph's tale is a testament to the disruptive power of foresight, determination, and leadership – qualities that echo through time, inviting us to embrace our own journeys with courage and innovation.

LEADING SELF

SELF-LEADERSHIP, taking individual responsibility, is paramount when navigating periods of uncertainty. You need to be unequivocal about your purpose and motivation, and about aligning your personal values with organizational objectives.

Before you can lead yourself, you need to know yourself. You need to understand your strengths, weaknesses, opportunities, and threats using the SWOT analysis framework. You need to meticulously assess your skills set and undergo a comprehensive life audit.

You also need to have a deep understanding of your company's policies in order to effectively navigate your way through the organization.

One of the most valuable pieces of advice I received from a former boss before starting a new role at the company was to thoroughly read the

Annual Report. She initially sent it to me via email, and upon my arrival, she provided me with a hard copy. I was able to gain a comprehensive understanding of the company's operations, and the vision that underpinned key decisions. Your understanding of where your company is headed is essential to your career success within it.

By taking ownership of your career journey, you can strategically assess your capabilities and areas for improvement. This introspective process not only enhances personal development but also empowers you to align your skills with organizational goals. In the face of sudden change, your ability to lead yourself helps you to be resilient and adaptable, and able to respond proactively to the challenges at hand.

You will experience fear and doubt during a sudden change, but it is important not to allow those emotions to overwhelm you or put you in a state of paralysis. Harness the power of fear to heighten your awareness of the situation and allow it to drive you to study and to be better equipped. Doubt, on the other hand, can be debilitating. It slows down one's thinking and can result in inaction, thereby hindering progress. Don't give in to doubt.

Getting feedback from others is a good way to lead self also. There are many tools that one can use for this. Recently I was introduced to the Johari Window Model. By utilizing this model, you can uncover potential blind spots and receive external input, enhancing your ability to lead ourselves effectively. It's essential to view feedback as a valuable gift, echoing Ken Blanchard's wisdom that "Feedback is the breakfast of champions." Complete self-leadership requires embracing feedback. The combination of inward reflection and external input will help you process the change and to react appropriately. In times of sudden change, the strategic use of external feedback becomes paramount.

THE SEVEN ELEMENTS

IN ORDER TO thrive while experiencing sudden change, you need seven key elements:

1. Know what you have in your hand.
2. Leverage the power of your network.
3. Have an endgame mindset.
4. Understand the time in your career timeline.
5. Have resilience and grit.
6. Seek the influence of mentors and coaches.
7. Envisioning the Future.

1. Know What You Have in Your Hand

The first element involves being aware of what you possess in terms of knowledge and talents. Your educational background and ability to absorb knowledge is critical in being prepared for sudden change.

You need to conduct a thorough assessment of the wealth of knowledge, experiences, and skill sets you have amassed in the course of your life journey. This involves not only recognizing your current strengths but also contemplating other skills that you possess that may be crucial in the future landscape. For those who are new to the workplace, your experiences at school play a huge part in determining what makes you you.

For instance, skills that are considered essential today in the field of software development might be obsolete tomorrow. Having the foresight to acquire skills such as understanding generative AI (Artificial Intelligence) APIs (Application Programming Interface) of the future can be a game-changer. By taking stock of your existing competencies and discerning the evolving needs of your industry, you not only sidestep future panic but you also arm yourself with indispensable tools for adeptly navigating and managing sudden changes on your professional horizon.

Believing in yourself and your abilities is also key during times of change. Despite what others may say, it is important to remember that skills and talents have brought you this far and can take you even further.

2. Leverage the Power of Your Network

Networking is another important skill you need to manage sudden change. It is often said that your network determines your net worth. Building and leveraging a strong network can lead to valuable opportunities.

I highly recommend LinkedIn as the place to go to build your network. LinkedIn is seen by many as a key global professional networking platform.

Start by understanding who is currently in your network and who you want to be in your network. Connect with peers, mentors, and others who can help you in your career. Make connections that will strengthen your network. Learn from your network, and give back to your network by helping others.

Networking is not just for extroverts. You can be an introvert and still build a powerful network that serves you well. The key point is that you must be intentional about building a network that is aligned to your career plan.

People often wonder what to do if they don't find joy in connecting with others. My advice is to give it a shot. Building a network doesn't require a multitude of connections, but rather, it's about finding the right people. Leveraging LinkedIn can be a valuable way of reaching out and establishing connections with professionals in your specific field.

Networking can also be done offline. Make a conscious effort to connect with people at events, conferences, or social circles. In the 1980s, people had a device called a Rolodex, which was a filing system for business cards, to organise the hundreds of cards they amassed from meetings and events. People who did not have a Rolodex had an address book with plastic pockets for storing their collection of business cards.

It doesn't really matter how you do it, start building your network today so that when sudden change happens you have people to call on. And if you already have a network, take steps to strengthen your connections.

Growing Your Network with the help of HR Professionals

Human Resources professionals have an important role in helping employees understand that an individual's network is a dynamic asset that contributes significantly to their professional net worth.

Building a robust network is like cultivating a garden of possibilities. The quality and diversity of relationships is more important than the number of contacts. In times of change, whether it be a sudden career shift or a broader transformation in the professional landscape, your network becomes a reservoir of support, insights, and opportunities.

A well-nurtured professional network serves as a safety net during turbulent times, providing a platform for knowledge exchange, mentorship, and collaborative problem-solving. It opens doors to unforeseen opportunities and widens the scope of possibilities. Through strategic networking, individuals can gain access to valuable advice, potential job leads, and even partnerships that may not have been possible through traditional channels.

Moreover, the reciprocal nature of networking fosters a culture of mutual support. Encouraging employees to actively engage in networking, both within and outside the organization, becomes a proactive strategy for managing change from an HR point of view. It not only enhances individual adaptability but also fortifies the overall organizational resilience. By recognizing and harnessing the true potential of networking, you empower individuals to transform their connections into a currency of opportunities, making them better equipped to thrive in the dynamic landscape of their careers.

3. Have an Endgame Mindset

It's also essential to have an endgame mindset and know where you want to end up in your career. What's your one-year plan? What's your five-year plan? What's your endgame plan? Knowing your "why" and defining what matters most to you can help guide your career path. To help you gain clarity on your goals, I recommend reading books like Simon Sinek's "Start With Why", seeking out a mentor, or mind mapping your life story.

Knowing your end game is critical to effectively managing sudden career transitions. As they say, "Plan for the plan." Embracing end game planning and cultivating an end game mindset are indispensable tools in your career journey. Consider Joseph in the Bible; his clarity regarding the end game informed his steps. We can learn so much from his wisdom.

Having a comprehensive game plan will help you to address unexpected shifts or setbacks. You need a crystal-clear vision of your objectives and a steadfast commitment to leveraging all available resources to attain them.

Mentors and coaches can provide you with invaluable guidance to help devise your end game plan. We will talk more about mentors and coaches in the next section.

This end game plan gives you context and helps you repurpose and pivot fast when experiencing sudden change. It's through challenges and changes that we often find our greatest opportunities for growth.

4. Understand the Time in Your Career Timeline.

Another important ingredient to mapping out your end game plan is to develop a deep understanding of your professional footprint over your entire career. You need to understand how your efforts have helped to shape your organization's success, as well as the ripple effects of your work on the wider community.

This will reveal your underlying motivation, which in turn will help you define your endgame strategy with a greater degree of clarity. Your underlying motivation is the secret sauce that propels you to your next career and life destination with unwavering determination. When you realise this level of clarity, you're not just in the end game; you're also defining your competitive edge.

A nuanced understanding of your career trajectory will better equip you to manage sudden change. The insights that you gain from this deep work will help you understand at what stage you are in your professional journey; are you at the nascent or beginning stages? Are you firmly entrenched? Or are you approaching the twilight of your career?

Having this knowledge will influence your priorities, and determine your response to abrupt transformations within your professional sphere.

To illustrate, people in their forties or fifties may be primarily preoccupied with the notion of leaving a legacy and effecting profound impact through their work. Conversely, younger people just starting off on their career journey may be more willing to embrace risk and actively pursue opportunities for skill acquisition.

A recent graduate, who encounters the unexpected setback of redundancy in their initial employment experience, will inevitably view such circumstances through the lens of an incipient professional voyage, potentially reevaluating their aspirations and objectives accordingly. An older person with several years of professional experience is likely to have a different outlook.

Understanding where you currently reside on your career trajectory will help you determine your next steps towards reaching your endgame. Therefore, you must set aside time for deep introspection and contemplation.

These moments help you to strategically assess your position and chart a meaningful course in alignment with your evolving career ambitions.

If your ultimate goal is retirement, your response to sudden change will not be the same as if your ultimate goal is to reach a certain level of success within your organization.

Aligning your career path with your aspirations and values is crucial for long-term satisfaction and success. When your work is meaningful and resonates with your core beliefs, you are more likely to stay motivated and find fulfillment in your achievements.

Ultimately, understanding your endgame plan, building a strong network, and knowing where you are on your career timeline are all important elements in successfully managing change in your career. By staying proactive and adaptable, you can navigate unexpected shifts with confidence and continue to grow and thrive in your professional life.

5. Have Resilience and Grit

Resilience is the capacity to swiftly rebound from setbacks and effectively adapt to change. Having resilience allows one to thrive in the face of adversity. A resilient person maintains a positive outlook on life, and adopts strategies to manage stress and navigate challenges.

Grit, on the other hand, can be defined as having the tenacity to persist and remain steadfast in pursuit of long-term objectives, even when confronted with obstacles and setbacks. It is a dynamic blend of passion and unwavering perseverance, serving as a driving force that keeps individuals dedicated and resolute in their journey toward achieving their goals. Grit can also be defined as unyielding determination

Resilience and grit are crucial components of a successful career. By combining these two traits, you push through adversity and achieve your goals.

I vividly recall receiving a WhatsApp message from my boss while navigating my way through a redundancy from a previous company: "I see you managed this transition with remarkable resilience." she remarked. In response, I expressed my gratitude and added that it wasn't just resilience but a mix of both resilience and grit working in tandem.

When you find yourself facing a career challenge, resilience and grit are potent tools to guide you toward a more promising "next" chapter.

In essence, by incorporating foresight, resilience, and unyielding determination (grit) into your career planning process, you can navigate the complexities of the professional world, overcome challenges, and create a meaningful and enduring impact within your chosen domain.

It is important to keep your gaze fixed on your

endgame and craft a strategic plan that harmonizes with your aspirations and values, you can attain success and establish a lasting legacy within your chosen domain.

Establishing a lasting legacy involves leaving a meaningful imprint on your field through your contributions, innovations, or mentorship. Aligning your career path with your aspirations and values is crucial for long-term satisfaction and success. When your work is meaningful and resonates with your core beliefs, you are more likely to stay motivated and find fulfillment in your achievements.

6. Seek the Influence of Mentors and Coaches

Having a mentor or a coach is particularly significant during periods of sudden change in one's career. These mentors and coaches assume distinct yet complementary roles, forming a dynamic support system that goes beyond the traditional boundaries of professional development.

Mentors, distinguished by their wealth of knowledge and expertise, serve as beacons of guidance and wisdom. They go beyond merely imparting information; a good mentor is able to recognize the latent greatness within an individual, and actively works to bring it to the forefront. They are able to share from their wealth of relevant experience, revealing shortcuts to help mentees reach their destinations more efficiently. Drawing inspiration from John C. Crosby's words, mentors serve as a source for advice, a willing ear for listening, and a motivating force, gently pushing individuals in the right direction. Their value lies in being knowledgeable, resourceful and compassionate listeners and motivators, steering mentees towards the correct path.

Coaches, on the other hand, bring a practical and methodical approach to the table. Coaches are able to provide actionable and effective methods and tools to identify and close skills and knowledge gaps. Beyond skill assessments, coaches build your confidence and self-esteem, and help you believe that you can become a better version of yourself. A coach will act as a guide to individuals or teams as they journey towards their goals, by getting involved in the details and having regular check-ins.

The combination of a mentor's insightful guidance and a coach's practical strategies results in a powerful support system during times of change. Together, coaches and mentors equip you with the tools you need to not only navigate the uncertainties of your career but to also proactively shape your path towards growth and accomplishment. In essence, the mentor-coach dynamic is a cornerstone upon which you build resilience, adaptability, and continuous improvement in your professional journey.

7. Envision the Future

When navigating a sudden career change, you need to anticipate and envision the future you want. This will help refocus your mind and counter the feelings of disorientation and loss.

Mentors and Coaches can be a great help in helping you to process your loss and envision your future. They play a crucial role in providing invaluable insights for the way forward.

While working as a security guard, I held a vivid mental picture of the future that I desired. This served as a constant force propelling me onward. I recognised that my current position was not my final destination and this knowledge propelled me forward.

Your End Game plan, in essence, acts as your driving force, while resilience and grit are the compass that steer you towards the envisioned future. It's imperative to cultivate a distinct image of the future that transcends the present, spanning one, five, and even ten years into the future.

This clear, forward-looking perspective is essential to realising your ultimate goals. When you are able to envision a pathway to a promotion or a lateral move, it infuses you with great strength to keep pressing forward. The power of mental visualization is profound — it allows you to pull forward toward your goals. Recall the biblical story of Joseph; his unwavering image of what lay ahead sustained him through life's challenges. What may seem impossible in the present, gains clarity through a vivid visualization of the future. Embrace this transformative perspective as you navigate your journey.

You may be wondering, how do you go about envisioning a new future? What kind of future should you anticipate? How do you guide your mind toward a brighter tomorrow?

In my experience, reading extensively has been the key to unlocking the potential of my mind. Every page of a carefully selected book, moved me a step closer to the future I desired. I typically read 15 - 20 books per annum on a range of topics pertinent to my walk. I read books by authors who I respect and who have achieved something that I aspire to or who are thought leaders on a relevant topic.

I also find inspiration in nature. I like to take long walks and there is something about the beauty and wonder of the natural world that ignites the creative spark within, and helps you imagine a vibrant and inspiring future in technicolour.

So, in your quest for clarity regarding the future, I invite you to embrace the power of knowledge. Read, read and read again. Also take time to experience and contemplate nature first hand. These two practices will help you chart your course towards a future filled with possibilities.

Another powerful practice is that of saying your vision out loud. Describe your vision to yourself and to trusted people around you in vivid detail. What colour is it? What shape is it? How does it feel? Then watch as every fiber of your being aligns to set you on a remarkable journey toward the picture in your mind. Unleash the unstoppable force within your subconscious that propels you towards your desired future. Your words and thoughts act as guiding lights, illuminating the path to your extraordinary destiny.

Doing this as a matter of course means that when sudden change happens you are equipped with a subconscious compass that will act as your guide.

See it, believe it, speak it, and watch your life unfold in alignment with the inspirational future you have crafted in your subconscious.

CONCLUSION

NAVIGATING SUDDEN CHANGE is akin to learning the steps of an intricate dance. In this book we have delved into the complexities and nuances that define these pivotal moments.

Unexpected shifts in employment can result in complete realignments of career trajectories. The impact of such changes extends beyond the individual and can affect industries, organizations, and even global events.

We have highlighted the need for adaptation, emphasized the importance of learning new skills, redefining roles, and embracing the potential for fresh beginnings. Sudden Change demands not only agility but a reflective and proactive approach to effectively navigate the uncertainties that lie ahead.

However, while sudden change can bring with it the potential for growth, we must also acknowledge the challenges inherent in a sudden change.

Everyone's experience is unique, and adjustment periods vary, resulting in both positive and negative outcomes. We must recognise that sudden change is a personal journey. There will be a diversity of responses and there will be a need for tailored strategies.

We talked about the power of strong networks, and how your network can be likened to your professional net worth.

Building and leveraging your network can open doors to valuable opportunities, offering support, insights, and collaborative problem-solving. From digital platforms like LinkedIn to offline networking at events, the significance of a strong network is highlighted.

We talked about crafting an endgame mindset, and underscored the importance of knowing where you want to end up in your career. Understanding your purpose, setting clear goals, and planning for the long term are essential components. The story of Joseph from the Bible serves as a poignant reminder that sudden change demands adaptability, creativity, and a willingness to challenge the norm.

Resilience and grit emerged as critical traits for navigating career challenges. Resilience allows for swift rebounding from setbacks, while grit ensures tenacity and perseverance in the pursuit of long-term objectives. The fusion of these traits becomes a dynamic force that equips individuals to thrive amidst adversity.

Mentors and coaches play a pivotal role in this journey. A mentor, recognizing greatness, provides guidance and shortcuts based on their experiences. A coach, with practical advice and methodologies, helps identify skill gaps and fosters confidence, nurturing individuals to become better versions of themselves.

As we conclude this exploration, we recognize that sudden changes are not merely disruptions but opportunities for profound growth. By embracing adaptability, nurturing networks, fostering an endgame mindset, and embodying resilience and grit, you can not only weather the storms of change, but you can emerge stronger and more resilient, ready to seize new opportunities on your professional journey.

Managing sudden change can be a challenging experience, but with patience, grit, resilience, and courage, it is possible to navigate through it successfully.

Remember, managing sudden change can be a challenging experience, but with time, patience, grit and resilience and courage you can successfully navigate through it.

Recommended Reading

1. Betting on a Darkie by Mteto Nyati tells the story of a successful CEO's journey through multiple sudden changes in South Africa.

2. The Art of Managing Up for Career Progression by Olusola Osinoiki, tells my career story and how I was able to manage my managers to achieve my career goals.

REFLECTIONS

How I Navigated a Sudden Career Change and Unexpected Challenges
- *Victor Olushola Kehinde*

I have over a decade of experience in my career as an enterprise network engineer and entrepreneur. I successfully managed multi-million dollar projects and served as a field associate in Nigeria for two, US-based, not-for-profit organizations. In this role, I advocated for the adoption and deployment of an electronic library system, facilitating access to over 40 million educational materials via a local area network without internet connectivity. With a thriving IT company and a team of 15, including remedial staff, I was living the dream of a successful entrepreneur and consultant, earning in dollars and enjoying great connections to society's crème de la crème.

However, my wife's aspiration to pursue a career as a university lecturer in Physics prompted discussions about relocating abroad for a master's program. As a young and promising entrepreneur with great connections in Nigeria and my industry, it was a huge mental struggle to accept or accommodate the thoughts of leaving such a life.

However, despite my established network in Nigeria and the success I enjoyed in my field, the economic and security challenges in the country eventually persuaded us to make the move to the UK in early 2022. The intention was to shuffle between Nigeria and the UK so I could continue to do business and see to other valuable engagements.

However, balancing my family's needs, seeing to recurring monthly bills, and caring for our three year old young son after school, due to limited after-school childcare became a priority.

Our new life in the UK came with unforeseen financial responsibilities, and led me to recognize gaps in my skills set. I decided to enroll on courses to enhance my expertise in product ownership and scrum mastery. After three months of diligent effort, I secured a Business Analyst role with the flexibility of remote work.

Adjusting to the dynamics of being an employee after years of entrepreneurial independence presented significant challenges. I navigated the shift from managing my own time and team to reporting to line managers and senior executives. The fear of job insecurity and the pressure to meet stakeholder expectations tested my resilience.

Through this experience, I gleaned invaluable lessons about adaptability and resilience. It helped me understand that unforeseen challenges may necessitate a fresh start in life or career. I learned the importance of managing upwards to remain motivated and positive. Despite the abrupt changes, I remained committed to creating value for my company and continued to explore entrepreneurial opportunities if circumstances demanded.

How I Navigated a Sudden Career Change and Unexpected Challenges
- *Kitan A.*

I have experienced my fair share of sudden career changes. The suddenness of these changes were however not driven by my non-participation in the decisions to move but more on the shock that lay on the other side of my decisions.

I remember how eagerly I had sought to move up the career ladder into a management position. After a few months of looking, I finally landed a role that I was certain was in line with my career goals. Technically, I was ready, I had worked hard to sharpen my leadership and management skills in order to be able to take up a role like this. However, the role and indeed the company, did not have the structures I was used to in my previous organisation. It felt like going from driving Tesla to having to drive a bus from the 80s. Not only did I have the responsibility of leading multiple sub-functions, managing direct reports, designing and implement-ting key structural changes, I also had to keep the wheels of this creaky bus moving.

Now how did I manage this situation and come out of it with a stellar report and a relationship with the company and my boss that is still strong?

1. I had documented why I wanted to move, and I kept myself motivated by my why.

2. I quickly assessed the situation and hatched a plan that would give me quick wins whilst trying to ensure no critical errors were made in other areas.

3. I acquainted myself with the company's history and its people. That gave me a lot of perspective on the state of affairs, and it helped me to proffer solutions that were practical and effective. Relationships developed across board and this made the implementation of new initiatives largely successful.

4. I took time to understand what was critical for the executive team and prioritised those tasks in order to ensure that their goals were top on my list. That way, I had the executive support that I needed to be successful.

5. I was in frequent communication with my mentor and was able to draw on his wealth of experience. He gave insightful suggestions and was also a major pillar of support in ensuring that I was successful in my first management role. He kept me accountable and focused on the big picture.

6. Finally on the few occasions where things didn't pan out correctly, I was very quick to take responsibility, pivot where necessary and always communicated with my key stake-holders.

Overall, the experience I gained from this role helped me to manage other changes that I have subsequently had in my career, and it serves a reminder of what can be achieved with a positive, problem-solving, company-focused and people-centred mindset.

REFLECTIONS AND COMMENTS BY REVIEWERS

HR can have a significant role in helping employees navigate unforeseen changes.

Proactively, they can develop programs or ini-tiatives throughout the employee life cycle that foster confidence and resilience. Examples include self-development, management, internal mentoring programs, wellness initiatives, coaching, and add-ressing unconscious bias.

However, in my experience, when abrupt changes like layoffs happen, HR often faces time constraints and follows a scripted communication process. The urgency and legal considerations during negative changes may limit the extent to which HR can pro-vide assistance or support.

– Inspired by Rumbidzai Muteswa

In the unpredictable landscape of professional life, it's the ability to navigate setbacks with poise and resilience that not only preserves one's professional standing but propels them toward greater achieve-ments.

– Ndimofor Aretas